The Observation Car

The Observation Car

Alan Brownjohn

HUTCHINSON
London Sydney Auckland Johannesburg

© Alan Brownjohn 1990

The right of Alan Brownjohn to be identified as Author of this work has been asserted by Alan Brownjohn in accordance with the Copyright, Designs and Patents Act, 1988

This edition first published in 1990 by
Hutchinson

Century Hutchinson Ltd, Random Century House,
20 Vauxhall Bridge Road, London SW1V 2SA

Century Hutchinson Australia (Pty) Ltd
20 Alfred Street, Milsons Point, Sydney 2061, Australia

Century Hutchinson New Zealand Limited
PO Box 40–086, Glenfield, Auckland 10, New Zealand

Century Hutchinson South Africa (Pty) Ltd
PO Box 337, Bergvlei, 2012 South Africa

British Library Cataloguing in Publication Data
Brownjohn, Alan, *1931–*
  The observation car.
  I. Title
  821.914

  ISBN 0–09–174456–3

Set in Linotron Times 10/12pt by Input Typesetting Ltd, London
Printed and bound in Great Britain by Cox and Wyman Ltd,
Reading, Berks

i.m.
C.H.B.

Acknowledgements

are due to the following, in which these poems, or versions of them, have previously appeared: *Agenda*, BBC Radio 3, BBC Radio 4 (*Time for Verse*), *Causley at 70* (ed. Harry Chambers), *Encounter*, *Equivalencias*, *Gown*, *Infolio* (ed. Tom Raworth), *London Magazine*, *New Statesman*, *Orbis*, *PEN New Poetry II* (ed. Elaine Feinstein), *Poems for Shakespeare 1988* (ed. Charles Osborne), *The Poetry Book Society Anthology 1987–1988* (ed. Gillian Clarke), *Soho Square 2* (ed. Ian Hamilton), *Spectator*, *The Times Literary Supplement*.

Part of 'A Tribesman's Dream', with the title 'Heard in a Dream', was published in *First and Always: Poems for Great Ormond Street Children's Hospital* (ed. Lawrence Sail).

Contents

SEA PICTURES

1

A man is bicycling along the sands,
Predicting the firm stretches where his wheels
Will not sink down; he listens to their hiss
As all the waves of the sea push towards him
In amenable ripples. He rode here down a lane
Where September offered all colours of blackberry
At the same time; at the dunes he lifted up
His vehicle over the gorse; and on the beach,
He set it down and pedalled off westwards.
He notices the boat far out, its windows,
Its smoke, and the man and woman on the sundeck.
When the boy turned and lashed out with his spade

2

At his aggravating sister, what could they do
But condemn him to stay and guard the clothes?
So the rest of the family, sister included,
Who would, in the boy's opinion, not have suffered
The same indignity had she swung the spade,
Make tracks towards the distant recession of waters,
Ignoring the tears which are flooding down over
His abolished castle. And then, double spy, Sod's Law,
He is stung by a wasp, and his older brother
Has to sprint back and see why he is roaring.
He comforts him; and picks up his dropped spade.
There was once a woman absolutely averse

3

To having her name romantically inscribed
On the sands, it was better to have it called
Romantically over the waters. And this dread
Of having even the letters of that word
Dispersed by the tide was one of her variants
Of the fear of death. But the elder of the two boys
Hasn't heard of such reluctance, he takes the spade
The smaller one is bored with, seeing it builds
No castles by itself, and begins to write
Some initials on a wide, firm, yellow stretch
Twenty yards or so away from the family clothes.
'The broughams of legitimate love' which the classic

4

Novelist[1] saw, are out this afternoon,
Creatures of slow and polished habit, getting
The best of the warmth of mid-September where
A line of them has poised itself sedately
Along the clifftop, windscreens to the sun
Which glints as well on countless points far out
On the surface of the not-too-restless sea,
Towards which in the distance a family
Of discontented people slowly treks.
At rightangles to them, behind them, a man
Will cross in one hour's time on a bicycle.
Two grandparents from one brougham see the two boys

5

As they gaze down from a clifftop rail the Council
Is still allowed to paint; and notice too
The boat almost stationary in the water

Half-way up to the horizon, though they can't see
The man still on the sundeck. In their boot
Are the blackberries taken from where they parked
In a safe straight lane, turned on their hazard lights,
Went round and checked the handles of every door,
And picked with plastic bags along the hedges,
While the dog sat mutely up in its barred-off space
And imagined human reasons for doing this.
In a cabin of the ferry, the woman lets

6

The door close behind her, having come back down
From the sundeck leaving the man; and she gives
This worried frown to herself in the mirror,
And goes hard at the problem of her hair,
All fraught and fixed and clenched by the attentions
Of only a slight breeze, with a honey-coloured
Comb. It needs to be coaxed, she needs to be coaxed,
But the engine beat is steady, the sea quiet,
And she balances easily. She is happy
With the spray that rinses her window, and decides
To take the camera with her when she goes.
'They are unloading coal at that small seaport

7

'Exactly – *there*!' The man has entered, starting
An uneasy conversation, and they both look
Through the window at an old tub releasing
An irregular cargo of brownish stuff
In rumbling slopes and screes as it creaks and stirs
In the harbour waters; holidaymakers watch.
'They say that coal has come from India,'
Unloading in the profound September sun

3

Which day by day seems more impervious
To the onset of autumn, as the woman's hair
Seems impervious to the corrections of her comb.
A sign made of coloured bulbs is saying 'Arnold's',

8

The name of an *Amusements* coffee bar
With machines which wink and flash, and thrust out tokens
Exchangeable for refreshments. Girls stand round
In leather, smoking Marlboro cigarettes;
Approaching from the quayside one hears the beat
Thumping out in the heavy haze; and Arnold stands
At a screeching urn not letting his poker-stare
Relax above the dull glass cups he fills
With cappuccino, sliding them across
To boys with mousey forelocks who eff and blind
So the leathery girls can't fail to overhear.
Plugged into his radio, Arnold, late one night

9

Heard something he would struggle to describe
For years: this heavenly voice with a colossal
Orchestra behind it, singing, it sounded like
Paradise, he would give his right arm to know
What it was that woman sang, he could hear, like,
The sea in it. Arnold, a fixture here,
Travelled far when the voice on the radio sang
On that long-ago night when the light was out
Above the rabies notice on the quay,
And the quay was deserted, and the harbour
Filling with ripples from Scandinavia.
A fly neglects its hindlegs but cleans its forelegs

10

On a burst éclair in one of Arnold's stands,
In the window fronting onto the quay where coal
Came on shore to the detriment of honour.
For a 10p coin in a slot, a painted donkey
Will jerk and shake to persuade a child to smile,
And elsewhere Arnold has arranged for aged
Citizens, senior and vulnerable,
And none of them the owners of broughams of love,
To have bingo played on them. Everyone
Gets something at Arnold's, and Arnold is content
Notwithstanding the cry of the singing in the night.
Back on deck the woman tries to remember where

11

She rode along on a high bus above amazing
-ly wide unvisited beaches, with roaring winds
And breakers all the summer, and free of footprints,
And tries to think why it is the selfsame spaces
Should feel forbidden now, you could not visit
To draw initials or ride a bicycle,
Or paddle through a dangerous undertow.
It wasn't the Black Sea coast or the Indian Ocean,
But somewhere nearer, though certainly not so near
As the littorals blessed by the patron saint
Of seacoast adulteries, St Lascivia.
When you go out through the archipelago

12

The first of the islands are amply inhabited,
With councils and roads and elaborate traffic signs.
And then the small towns are large villages,

And the villages dwindle down to sociable clusters
Of one or two small red houses, though even now
In these you sometimes spot a post-box bearing
The logo of the royal mail. Then finally,
By which time it is dark even on their sundeck,
The lights are from single cabins on single rocks
With one boat tethered in a cranny, the last
Places of all they might remember you.
'Tell me about them later, I'd like to take

13

'A photograph of that man on the bicycle.
And what was the boy's game writing those initials?'
'It wasn't a game, and don't take a photograph.
I wanted to tell you how I felt just like Arnold
When I was staying on the Black Sea coast:
In an adjacent room of the hotel,
The cleaners were making the beds up and a radio
Was transmitting an opera. Through the open door
The baritone was filling the corridor,
A resonant, yearning, echoing baritone,
And at once I knew I should never forget the sound.
A dog was lying on the esplanade,

14

'And I had the sense, standing there by the window,
Of being at the edge of a still from an Eastern
European film, and not real. And I knew this feeling
Would be an always reachable memory;
Especially as I couldn't exactly tell
If the dog on the esplanade were alive or dead.
Some men were now approaching with what looked like
A sack, to pick it up. Yet when I joined

6

The woman at her own window on the next floor
Five minutes later, dog and men were gone,
And she hadn't seen any of this at all.'
'Why don't you want me to take a photograph?'

15

'Because too many photographs are a problem;
All those quotidian dull remembrancers.
Myself, I keep a cache of a special few
In a hidden envelope somewhere. There is one
Of myself in the middle distance jogging
Along a wide yellow beach, and another
Of a jumble of roughly teddy-bear-shaped
Concrete blocks, sea-defences at Constanţa,
Both examples being taken on sunny days
When no wasp was stinging and, in general, Sod
Was happy to suspend his evil Law.'
Writing images for people to come across

16

Is like swearing to attract attention, but more
Effective because more people notice it;
And when you have overheard an image it makes
A deeper difference. I couldn't get away
From the images of the dog and the baritone
Romantically affirming in unknown music,
With all the power of long experience,
That love was a province of maturity
(Anton Walbrook playing Hoffmann[2] in *The Tales of*,
For example), not a hobby for adolescents.
It kept me listening, watching at my window.
Somewhere I read that Freud said, 'Civilization

'Is the postponement of gratification';
And for that reason I have put off learning
To swim until my sixties. I shall jog,
Which is rarely gratifying at the time,
Only later, when one still can run upstairs
In one's fifties, in that arsehole of the year,
The month of March. So, leaving the bicycle
Padlocked on a sandbank, I jog; and as I reach
The initials, waiting to be smeared out flat
By one repetition of the tide, I disagree
That writing them, the boy was up to a 'game'.
A man is jogging along the sands,

Predicting the firm stretches, which you can't tell
By their colour, only a dry and level look,
And by footsteps which barely mar the surface,
Though left by whole families. Sometimes the yellow sand
Looks hard, but it has still retained the water:
Don't plunge into that mushiness, or the going
Will get heavy-hearted, and your chest-bone ache
With a sinister burning as you plod on, and on.
Sand-patterns of corrugation are tough on
The soles of the feet, avoid those. And never try
To run much on loose sand, you simply won't.
Above the beaches of the Antrim coast

You could ride on high buses once, past cemeteries
Where plastic domes placed over tombstone wreaths
Protected them from the wind, and gaze far down

Across gaping bays of rock and untrodden sand
Where in recent years to leave a car might be
To have it detonated; fair enough.
And the idea of the North Antrim coast remained
As a reachable memory, kept safe somewhere
In a hidden envelope of the mind,
Not a photograph. To bring it out would be
Like replying at last to a standing invitation
Issued forty years before and never answered.
'If someone was feeling ill, or just confidential

20

'About the special one malaise which sent them
To the end of the archipelago, to the last
And smallest of twenty thousand solitudes,
They could still return.' And now the slow still moon
Was in silver pieces in the ferry's wake,
So they stacked up their conscientious chairs and went
Downstairs to the cabin and felt less landlocked
Than before, and were suddenly lovers.
'You should have let me take some photographs
Of the archipelago gradually turning
Into isolated seagull rocks,' she turned and said.
In their deep freeze the gathered blackberries make

21

The sexagenarians' equivalent
(Plucking them, hoarding them, discussing them)
Of the fruits once cherished by those who made
Libations at the shrine of St Lascivia.
She it is protects women who live on seacoasts
And feel a surge of forces wherever they face,
And know, where they live, they cannot be canutes;

9

These seacoast adulteries being most usual
When one participant lives by the sea (the woman)
And the man visits regularly from town.
[Their love involves this kind of fantasy.]
It has been known for two people living

22

In the same seaport to have an illicit liaison,
But St Lascivia does not hear their prayers.
They say she listens to the prayings of
The many others (if not the atheists,
Who get more done by hoping) who have to wait
For visitors from the city: that she keep
The crucial letters until the midday post
(Which doesn't get so much scrutiny), that she cause
The husbands' trains to be late if *they* are late home,
And have the restaurant's name and price erased
From the tell-tale credit card account.
I can remember nineteen forty-eight

23

As the year of walking the promenade at Eastbourne
On evening after evening, leaving aside
Their holiday and my parents to explore
With a sudden half-enjoyable loneliness,
The fantasy darkness under Beachy Head,
Where the sound of the band fades down and the
                                        bandstand lights
Are compressed into a clutter of distant stars.
Passing the neon signs: *Electric Lifts*
On modest small hotels, my mother (still able
To walk, and run, and even play tennis) wondered

10

Why electric lifts were considered such a boast.
I read *The Insect Play*, and in the bathroom

24

Mirror did not look like a butterfly:
Less colourful, less fragile, more permanent,
And happy in retrospect not to live in an age
Where people gaze into mirrors of butterflies
Reflecting only themselves, and never coal
Crashing down onto quaysides to carry power
To rooms where potted rubber plants are nourished
By hunger on a Coromandel coast.
'The boy was not playing a game with those initials,
But moving towards maturity, showing in sand
The postponement of gratification.'
At Mahabalipuram, remembering[3]

25

Louis MacNeice, the cows of sea-worn stone
Smile out at the sea, an extraordinary blue
With a freshness going out and on for ever,
But crashing back against a sudden shelving
Downwards of yellow sands in a crumbling bank
Beside the shrine, where they will sell you moonstones.
And the mile on mile passed parallel to the blue
In the bus back to the city held me close,
Scanning down to the Indian Ocean past sunburnt grass,
My first tropical coast, at fifty-seven,
Not to be jogged along or trifled with.
Someone had written in studs on the road in front

11

Of the great rock-carvings, the initials of
The strongest political faction to emerge
From the feuds after the death of MGR.
The letters were stamped into the carriageway:
DMK. The coaches driving across them
Made no difference, the sun glanced over them,
Beggars begged over them, and they were not erased.
On a wall, a rival face, Miss Jayalalitha[4]
(Called 'this film siren' by her enemies),
Who wept at the cortège of her dead lover.
She beat the Congress (I) into third place.
If I had to reveal the truth about the coal

Slipped into the little port, it was scab coal
Imported to beat the miners, and the year
Was nineteen eighty-four when the ferry passed
Along the coastline carrying them away,
The man and the woman becoming lovers
Somewhere beyond an archipelago.
She tugged her hair free, only half-listening,
But did take in the moral of the coal
As someone might have taken from a lover
Suez, or Vietnam, or the Falklands War;
And then resumed a lover's fantasies.
Here he is, writing initials on the beach,

And as he makes the furrows and smells the damp,
He yearns, which is what you do when you are mature.
This boy is using the sand as the first page

Of the very first poem he will ever write,
And what if it is only a *concrete* poem,
Or even a *language* poem, that is enough.
He has created something to show he feels,
And with the heart he draws around them *what*
He feels. But for decent reticence he does it
Twenty yards away from the clothes and his stung brother,
Who is not looking, weeping in the sand.
'After seeing the place where the dog might have been,

29

And wondering if there had ever *been* a dog,
I went into a strip-lit marble bathroom
Done in cold green, all elegantly Spartan,
Befitting a place where Ovid yearned for Corinna.
The sound of the opera might just have stopped,
Though I can hear it now, and see the sunlight,
And the shadows of the men on the esplanade.
I felt unreal because I was somewhere else,
On a foreign coast where foreigners stared far out
Into the deep prospect of Central Asia.
I wished I had thought to bring a camera.
If you stand on a day of sea-mist and look across

30

Any strait dividing two of the Scilly Isles,
You can believe the one you are looking at
Is very far away . . . separated from you
By a wide sea of rocks and ravaging currents;
It is a *trompe l'œil*. And in front of the man
Who bicycles along the Norfolk coast
Is the half-sunken wreck of a Second World War block ship,
A sight providing a similar illusion:

13

It seems miles off, but you can stroll out to it
And not see the incoming tide surround you,
Like a curtain hem let down by the horizon.
'I wonder what an Arctic coast is like,

31

'And how you know where the sea-edge (a remote
Conception of tides in a hunter's mind) ever is.
In landlocked countries the sea must be an idea
Culled from pictures, still ones or in motion,
A long, long way from Arnold's coral reefs;
Where languages have hardly any words
For "undertow" or "sea-mist" and can't translate
"Its melancholy, long, withdrawing roar".'
'You'd need to imagine the impossible, just as I
See you daily when you are nowhere near, and not
So close it seems a madness to be apart.'
Walking towards him down a long boulevard,

32

She arrives as they do in those dreams when you
Are an unseen being observing everyone,
And she walks right past him because it never makes
Any sense to think they could be in the selfsame street.
His thoughts have set her moving, staged an image
Of a glamorous and intricate machine
Gliding certainly and dangerously towards him
– And into the room where she becomes a presence
Like an incoming tide rewriting her,
Instead of erasing her like her initials
(Which are studded indelibly in his mind).
One day, nostalgically, in a hidden

Envelope, a man came across a photograph
Of his grandparents paddling from Margate to Ramsgate
Hand-in-hand with his father, the grandmother's left hand
Hanging on to a spade, while grandfather, farthest out,
Exhorts the trio forward through the ripples.
He knew his grandfather was a photographer
By those sepia pictures in the envelope
Hidden in a personal drawer; and yet he must
Have that day leased the camera to someone else
To take this picture; there has to be another
To capture those ancient people, and that girl.
In nineteen-o-seven you were not supposed

To move an inch, a fraction, especially ladies:
Photographs were a posed phenomenon,
And these three relations strolling the tideline foam
Eighty years ago had managed to hold the pose,
The boy's disconsolate look, grandfather's look,
And the movement of their ankles and their shins
Through the ridges of the incoming wet.
So they all slosh through a gentle undertow
Out of their early century, moving on
To assume their immortality somewhere else;
And grandfather gets a picture of the girl.
The grandmother's face in all these photographs

Is the indulgence of her husband's whim
Of trapping into a box the garden scenes,
The family groups, the walkers breasting tapes,

And the impending sea storms, lots of those,
Even though the very moment a lens cap
Is back in place, and the camera stored away,
The sunlit poses are turning sepia.
Photographs watch and watch the changes caused
By time, and trace them happening as surely
As the hour hand on the clock can be seen to move
If you follow it with sufficient concentration.
One night in a landlocked country, the owner of

36

A camera waits for the orange light to gleam
To tell him he can use the flash. He stands
In a city in a distant mountain province
Where the sea is rarely invoked in metaphor,
But where his inherited disposition
(A grandfather's whim) removes a lens cap in
A snow-filled street, and a woman in furs, in seconds,
Turns round on the ice, and balances, and smiles in the dark:
A set of images dangerous to put
In a hidden envelope found in the morning post;
And the smile and the darkness are both permanent.
The woman on the sundeck would have taken

37

A photograph of the single bicycle's tracks,
Inexplicable to walking families,
Who might grasp footprints or even horses' hoofs,
But can't see people ever *cycling* here,
Let alone applying the brakes to stop
And watch a ferry pass, as the man does now,
A prince at a ruined castle and some initials
Attaching to a girl by Lake Balaton,

Remembering a dog on a Black Sea strand
Unchained by death, and pausing here for breath
Before he jogs towards the one seagull rock.
When they stop looking, the man and the woman

38

With their boot full of blackberries on the clifftop,
Whose living dog gazes out between the bars,
The cyclist stops, with less than the certainty
Of someone who has cycled before today,
And more with the insecurity of someone
Who has rarely achieved a balance on his ride,
And is glad to be getting one foot firmly down
On the sand, and the other down beside it, and lean
On the handles of the vehicle, and keep
The twangling instrument upright while he stares,
While he stares far out to sea at the fixed clouds.
He is *all the daughters of his father's house*

39

And all the . . . He sees boys who write initials
Where only the waves will come across them
Grow into lovers bargaining on sundecks,
Losing their lens caps in Hungarian snow,
And turning round from clifftops to where the broughams
Have changed into hearses. Now I've reached the end
Of its interlacing tracks, I hold the bicycle
Cleverly upright with one steadying hand,
And space my feet for balance, and watch the sea:
The clouds, having settled where to rest, will not
Be moving again for the rest of the still day,
The waters have become an off-blue curtain

Let down by the horizon, and behind
This fabric something impels it, sways it . . .
The tide smooths down its shifting folds and layers
To touch me only as a small grey hem
Criss-crossing against the wheel I point at it,
And turning over into colourless,
Amenable ripples; but the wider air,
A huger, superseding element,
Fills everything with its roar, I can't make out
One wave or breeze to listen to for itself
In the general outcry, where I now observe
The boat sail out of sight, to vast applause.

Notes

1. *the classic/Novelist*: Balzac, in *History of the Thirteen*.
2. *Anton Walbrook playing Hoffmann*: the speaker in the poem is mistaken. The part of Hoffmann in the 1951 Powell and Pressburger film of Offenbach's opera was played by Robert Rounseville.
3. *At Mahabalipuram, remembering*: Louis MacNeice's 1948 poem with the title 'Mahabalipuram' may be found in his *Collected Poems* (ed. E. R. Dodds).
4. *Miss Jayalalitha*: her party won the second largest number of seats in the Tamil Nadu state elections of 1989, beating the Congress (I); but the DMK won the most.

SHORTER POEMS

Observation Car

At last they arranged it so that you just couldn't see
Out of any train window. You had to focus
On the back of the seat in front, or on the floor,
Or on the obligatory food, wheeled up on trolleys
To where they had strapped you in; though a favoured few
Could end up riding at the rear of the train
In the Observation Car,[1] from where the receding lines
Added ever-increasing length to the two sides
Of an angle wedging acutely into the past.
How fast that terrain seemed, and interesting,
Though it vanished before you guessed it had ever been:
You saw your bridges after you had crossed them,
You learned what was before you saw it coming,
And everyone pointed and said, 'The amazing things
We were missing all that time! If we had known,
We might have stopped the train and got out to enjoy them.'
– In this assuming they were better off
Than the others, sitting boxed in their airline seats
And observing nothing. When occasionally
Someone tried to complain to the guardian who came
Down the gangway cancelling tickets, he would say,
'You are fortunate to have seats, either there or here,
In the midst of such a good metaphor for life.'

Note

1. The worst current example of the phenomenon described is the
French TGV, where every resource of locomotive technology has
been dedicated to passenger-imprisonment; making it possible, for
example, to travel from Paris to Geneva and see nothing at all of
the landscape for which you chose the train instead of the plane.

September Days

When I tap on the barometer, its needle
Flicks upward; but the year is rendering down.
It has grown too used to itself to last for long,
And has to be content with doing gracefully
The things it can't avoid. I look up,

And those clouds block the sun for hardly a minute
More than they did a week ago, in the summer;
And when they move, the scene can seem to be
As juvescent as ever. But when I move
Through this gap in the hedge, I start some pheasants

Going off like motor-horns, sweeping away
Across an autumn haze of wheat-dust, lifted
From the cut fields by a high wind forcing
The grass and poppies into crestfallen curtsies.
Each day the month comes back with its shining face

A little more austere, with its shadows
Slightly longer and colder to step aside from
Into something like warm sunlight. The crops uncut
Are moving their heads now, like an applauding
Audience expecting someone to take a bow.

There is only me in this landscape. There was only me
This morning, in the brightness of the beach,
And I thought I still had strength to run against
Those droves of white sand raised by the same wind . . .
Should I bow, in winter's direction, like the grass?

Committal

I am waiting at the bus stop back to school,
But how on earth –? Nothing has ever changed,
Not the street, not the curtains in the houses . . .
This is the last hour of the holiday
Before the bell, an hour holding as much
Of freedom as I shall ever know. Somehow
I sense I shall never regain the sun
That shone on my breakfast things, back in that room
Five minutes ago. And what is she thinking,
My mother, as she clears them away? Does she want
Me to grow up or not to? What are her thoughts
As I leave her and, waving, she shuts the door?
What is there growing in the day for her?
By standing here I commit myself to worlds
Where no one will be proud of me with no reason.

Now the bus looms from the skyline, reaching me
With a top deck front seat vacant: Jupiter
Could sit up here 'gazing down from heaven's height'[1]
– Though that was last term's book. By the Plaza,
It takes a wide turn, passes the Hospital, drops
A few of us at the Library, and drives on.
I look back for one face (still there!); and now
I'm walking the wooded lane again to school.
And why do I now take my place with the others,
Still noticing the grain of the table, scored
Into rivers with compass points, all coloured blue,
While someone circles with this term's Shakespeare?
Of course I know already which play this is,
Its lines having thronged in my head most of the night . . .
If I open it when it comes, I commit myself.

How is it that I recognize the stains
On the old green cover, as it hangs in mid-air
Between him and me? I am waiting, watching
For the morning to start in the old, usual way:
For someone to start the jokes about the things
We might go in for: marriages, mistresses,
Ministries, either in Government or Church.
By ten o'clock we will have exorcised
The future I dream this in, and forgotten it.
Now the play glides towards me, and a voice
Is urging, whispering, 'Have it, hold it, feel
The weight of it, it's light, you'd not believe . . .'
So I take it. And the volume, like a rock,
Weighs my hand down, as it did last night before
I committed myself to forty years of sleep.

Note

1. '*Jupiter . . . gazing down from heaven's height*' construes Virgil,
Aeneid, Book I: *Jupiter aethere summo/Despiciens*.

In the Event

When the cat fled past like a running cushion
And vanished into the images on the screen,
I dropped my cup. The splash of coffee made
A wider stain on the flagstones than seemed
Quite possible, a large, seared cat-shape
We could not erase for some time. And the cup smashed.
So I said: Take the bits out into the garden
And deposit them with the rest. Our family is

Accustomed to recovering from the shock
If a fire recalls its burning, and the flames
Die back to kindling wood and unlit coals;
And accustomed to breaking a plate, or bowl, or dish
If one walks upstairs with it during a heat wave noon
And opens a bedroom window onto moonlit snow . . .
We have learned to be used to whatever happens here;
Which is why our garden is a rubbish trove
Of crockery pieces back to toga times
And beyond them, to broken arrows and fumbled flints.
So I said: Drop the fragments out in the garden,
And I will stroll along the long gallery,
Calling my ancestors severally out of their frames
To assemble on the terrace. In tall-heeled boots,
And buckled shoes, and sandals, and calloused feet,
They shall tread the patterned pieces into the ground.

What Lovers do in Novels

What lovers do in novels, day on day,
With changing amounts of patience, is wait and yearn.
When they can, they write letters, when they can,
They try to eat a little, or try to sleep.
And all the time they are reading other novels:

Novels which recount the techniques and agonies
Of waiting and yearning, and occasionally in ways
That bring hope.
           For example, here's a chapter
Where a lover sighs and lays a novel down,
Still open, on the leather arm of a chair,

And thinks (leaning deeply back, he thinks):
I have read through summer and autumn without
Consolation, nothing happens that I desire;
And yet I shall read along the shelf to where
My sorrow is found exactly, and understood;

Is found and rewarded, counted and repaid.
If I am hungry, if I cannot sleep,
If the telephone needs me, I shall still read on.
There has been a raggedness about my life
That a true and tidy fiction would trim back.

There is bound to be one novel which does all this.

All Best

I go with the grain of foreign courtesies
By writing, to somebody met only twice,
I remain, your impassioned eternal lover
Or *My soul is yours each minute of day and night.*
Inevitably, a laughing answer comes:
'No, no! It is all wrong. I tell you, please,
The words we are using here, and you will find
The nearest words in English to say it right.'

So for months all my letters begin and end
With ever more misjudged felicities,
Still striving to please correspondents for whom
I love you until death is no stronger than

Good morning, and for whom not to say,
In concluding the simplest thank-you letter,
I touch you all over, always, in my thoughts
Is tantamount to insult. It does not work.

I watch the leaves turn colour, at different speeds,
And start another letter wondering
Should I go back to intriguing understatement?
The kind I used once, coaxing long threads of hair
From between a pillow and the incomparable
Shoulders which trapped them, so as to release
A head and lips for a more than thank-you kiss
– When I only had strength enough for *kind regards*?

April Light

Slowly the tree falls, and we lean back
On our axes watching it, in the film,
Leaning on arm-rests in the Odeon.
The trunk and riven stump will kill nobody
In the good April daylight we had then.
So when the man with the name my friend had
Thirty years ago, and a credible address,
Dies today in the *Guardian*, struck by a falling tree,
This is fiction, it can't *be* him, it's a common name,
And trees fall commonly in reported storms.
So I don't go to the telephone, and I don't start
To write at last the letter I never wrote
When neglect was slowly cutting away at friendship.

I laugh at the idea, at the superstition,
And lean back in my chair, watching the light
Fall on a spring day killingly like winter.

A World of Pre-emptions

The time had arrived, a hermit thought, to be sociable
for a while, so the anchorite's existence would feel more of a
deprivation when he resumed it.

On the outskirts of the town, apparently, was a new
café, which advertised home-made flapjack on a leaflet left in
his cave-mouth. One sultry day the hermit decided to hang up
his silence, as a dog might its arse-hole, on a hook; and take
his savings of £5.90 (a note and small change); and go down
to see what the place was like.

His foot on the mat inside the door rang a bell, but the
waitress did not look up, only coughed over the confectionery
on her counter (she was beautiful to the hermit and he did not
mind). Before he could sign to her, or speak, she brought him
flapjack and lemonade as if she had already known his needs.

Two silent men in a corner might have played dominoes
had there been any to play; but they seemed content not to,
not wanting to vie with one another even in the maths of
chance.

And wonderful! – there was no canned music, so the

hermit was not distracted from the incidental colours and sounds: the heliotrope blouse of a woman stepping across to the Ladies; the clang of a roller-towel tugged down in its metal case moments later.

The waitress had had her ears pierced two days before; but all she had in them were two small brass rings, not the gleaming figments for which she had given herself to the operation. The hermit noticed and admired them; for him they were enough.

He watched the bubbles rising in his drink, and the legs rising in the skirt of the waitress. How he would deserve another decade of celibacy after observations like these!

Half an hour passed, and the sky clouded. The two men had left, carrying the quietness between them elsewhere, perhaps to the Central Station and a train to a distant village. The woman in the heliotrope blouse had left.

The waitress was clearing food into fridges and freezers and larders in a manner suggesting that closing time was near. The hermit's social moves would have to come soon.

A dry electric storm began outside. Thunder clapped and lightning forked, but there was a positive *coitus interruptus* of rain, which was unleashing elsewhere without drastic effect. The town was not prepared for rain, so the authorities had diverted it accordingly.

The hermit approached the counter with a short prepared speech. The light had turned the deepest blue. The windows were inky with the ulterior motives of the storm.

The hermit looked at the waitress and she at him. They

27

stared at each other with what he thought was the level, summatory gaze which can reach down into glands and gonads and start dynasties.

He wanted her to charge him, so he could be sociable about the transaction, hear his voice communicating with her so that his knowledge of all he was denying himself might be refreshed. And then the waitress just said, 'Ninety pence.'

'Ninety pence.' And because the hermit had the right money, there was no call even to say, 'I'm sorry I've nothing smaller.' He was without any speech of sociable information to give.

And he realised that this was a world of pre-emptions, where all desires were painlessly limited and fed before you even knew you had them. Every move received its countermove even before the game had been devised and marketed.

When he had decided to be a hermit, there had been no rock and no cave on the map; and yet, when he arrived in the town an agent found one to sell him, at a price.

There had been no café until the morning he felt the need to be sociable and found the leaflet in front of his cave.

As he left, hearing the doormat ring his departure, the waitress was unleashing the venetian blinds with a clatter, and shutting in the café lights for the night.

When the last blind was down and the last light gathered in, she pressed *Stop* and *Reject*, removed the cassette of the Music of the Spheres, and put it back for another ten years in the cardboard sweet box on the shelf marked 'Universal Fruits'.

A Dream of Launceston

for Charles Causley

So clear and safe and small,
on the nearest horn of
about twenty-seven

steady-breathing fellows
who have me cornered in
a field in North Cornwall

with their overbearing
friendliness (is it that?)
the ladybird allows

a petticoat of wing
and then recovers it.
And then: one pink-and-blue

nose lifts, and a deep note
rides out over the grass
to tremble the yellows

of the low primroses . . .
And 'Shoo' I say, and 'Shoo!'
in my nine-year-old voice

each time the dream comes back.
They do not shoo, and I
will not grow up, at all.

Reading the numbers on
the twitching ears as if
nothing more happened next,

I crave the freedom of
that tiny elegance
to flaunt itself, and fly.

An Ordinary Player

Today's choice for surgery glides past
With a wave and a request: 'Brass handles, please!'
The surgeon's lips will smile inside his mask,
The anaesthetist's hat is a perky white
Like a fast food chef's.
                          Late in the afternoon
He glides back, waking, as the January
Darkness renders us our long clean room
In coloured windows: blue sisters read
Our records, and a witness nurse stares down
At the red pills shaken in the dice-cup.

With the supper done, we shuffle up our chairs
To allow a space: including in the deal
One other player, to be entertained
Because he is too close for discomfort,
And far too ordinary to fend off
With superstition.
                     Still he has not won
When the ceiling lights dim out and the pictures fade,
And we return to bed, passing the table
Where the coloured pieces of the Monster
Puzzle lie half-unsolved in the half-dark.

Crossings

In hospital with the National Health, I see
A newspaper obituary for J.W. ('Jack')
Martin, Kent and England, easily our most
Impressive sporting Old Boy; and I'm intrigued
To find it's by Roy Fuller, friend from another
Sphere altogether. My south-east London school
Had just two famous sons, J.W.
Martin and Lord (John) Vaizey; though far back,
In the 1920s, Montague Summers taught there:
'A fine, distinguished man,' one master said,
Not gauging the sum of his reputation . . .

I see Jack Martin up at Whitefoot Lane,
The school sports ground, position a sly Point
Four feet from the Ist XI Captain
During Old Boys v. School; and duly bounce
First ball of the over, blithely, easily,
From pitch to bat to hand. Silenced, I stand
At the Debating Society that same week,
Thinking to make a case against the public
Funding of medicine, as left-wing Vaizey
Rises up blithely from the floor to place
A vigilant Point of Information . . .

Tristis

Though the room is lucid again, she actually dares
To hang around demanding to be a Muse.
No more than a gleam, a glitter, a scintillating
Wheel set alight by a hateful, hidden spark
– Does she think to inspire by being *that*?

Or by being the way the perspective in a street
Turns nonsensical? By jangling the print on a page
To a seething mix which hustles the book aside,
And forces me to sweat until her writhing
Steadies, and slowly settles, and switches off?

She always comes for free, she's saying, why don't
I pay her creative attention? I owe her that much.
And one day I'll miss her, she wheedles, this could be
The very last chance.
              I am tired. But you want it? I'll give it,
Your due recognition. Don't go. Stay and hear what you are:

A whore from the stews behind the ordered screen
Of everyday appearance, a short-time fix
Of dirty grey confusions, a half-hour drab
With a tawdry veil that shimmers.
                         Now you've taken
Your pound of spirit, feed and don't come back.

Secrets from and with

'Whirlpool closed for repairs'

At least we were seasick among friends

He who controls the photocopier controls the polytechnic

Religious Hats (a cigarette card series)

Amuse yourself sandpapering the new cathedral

Like musical chairs but adding a new chair every time
   the phonograph stops

Terminal, man. Your data stop here

Did you see that prostitute in a helmet going past
   the window?

The cows are chewing clockwise so we *must* be in the
   northern hemisphere

Can you tell me who lost the losers' race?

Moments of Hideous Indiscretion (a cigarette card series)

He was *disgusting*, Marie Lloyd said he was *disgusting*

And rose again on the third day the organ of the
   Granada Tooting

You've changed, you talk in noun clauses all the time

The last moral maxim going out of the other ear

Grow your beard up to your nose, pull your hat down over
         your eyes, shut your mouth and abstain as if
             you were voting

Are you a Gentleman, or a Player? – I am a Quantity
         Surveyor

Varieties of Post-coital Triste (a cigarette card series)

If you are on your death-bed, why are you doing a handstand?
         – To see the answer printed upside down.

A Brighton

'Brighton': not far, a lie or an excuse
Like dental checks or grandmothers' funerals.
'Did you have a nice day at Brighton?' asks the master
Receiving a boy's forged note about his cold.
The question is South-London-rhetorical,
A euphemism coined for the blind eye.

In Denver and Kanpur they have no Brighton,
No brief escapes to the fictitious sea.
The lovers say, 'If only there were in our lives
A Brighton, willing as an invented friend,
So people could allow that we went to the station
And saw the ticket clerk practise his knowing smile.'

A Tribesman's Dream

(from the legends of the F'kawi)

I

He has a
vision of the
Best People
in his
Culture, led
by their
Queen

I dreamt that I saw this woman, in front
Of a huge parade, she was marching her count-

ry's choicest spirits steadily
Into realms of opportunity:

There were judges, police chiefs, entire boards
Of directors, civil servants, hoards

Of entrepreneurs, intelligent
Trade unionists of a moderate bent,

Tabloid editors, turf accountants,
Expert management consultants,

Crisp-haired investment analysts
With micro-computers on their wrists,

Estate agents, merchant bankers,
Radical historians and think-tankers,
And advertisers and similar persons . . .

II

She is
dreadfully
disappointed
that some do
not live up to
Her
Example, and
do not
deserve Her.

But as she led and they followed in line
To glut themselves on her grand design,

She gazed around; and on every hand
There were people who did not understand!

– Councils, social workers, teachers,
Doctors, surgeons, embittered preachers

Who deemed it their spiritual task
Not to kneel and pray but to up and ask

Questions about the state of the nation,
And stir up a general aggravation

About the homeless, the sick and the poor;
So she said to them: 'You must take my cure

For a country slack with every sin,
And teeming with enemies within.
We must get things moving. And, to begin,

III

She converts
the Seven
Deadly Sins
into Saintly
Attributes

'We'll direct *Avarice* through a prism
To colour it like *Consumerism*;

And then give *Envy* a cleaner face
As *Competitiveness* – that's no disgrace;

Take *Sloth* from the class where it is the norm,
And give it to the rich as *Tax Reform*:

Move *Lechery* over into the *Sun*
As *Entertainment* for everyone;

Turn ravening *Gluttony* inside out,
There's a *Nose for Business* in every snout;

Tell *Anger* it may shoot to kill
As long as the gun is our *Regime's Will*;

And for a climax, raise private *Pride*
Into monstrous warheads, so to provide
For our country's *Strength* to be glorified.

IV

She will teach
the laggards
lessons in
handling their
affairs in
accordance
with Her
instructions

'As for the needy, the old and the lame,
They must learn the rules of a different game,

Where one basic principle applies,
The name of which is *Enterprise*.

If they have more nightmares than sweet dreams,
They can chase them away with private schemes,

They can count up their pennies and do their sums
And save for insurance premiums,

And if the dole and the benefit
Don't cover ten per cent of it,

That's not the job of the Commonweal,
It's for *Charity* to provide and heal

– You aren't with BUPA or PPP?
Oh that's neglect! That's infamy!
You'll have to depend on *Charity*.

V

She gives
them sound
advice and
some of Her
home truths

'Stop whingeing about "the money bags",
And get out there with your tins and flags,

Collect from the claimant-in-the-street
And tell him to stand on his own two feet,

Set up pub raffles and club bazaars
And ten-hour programmes with chat-show stars:

37

When it comes down to the nitty-gritty,
It's the widows' mites from the inner city

Must pay for their cardiac operations,
The responsibility is *not* the nation's . . .'

*   *   *

But the evil vision fades as the Queen, still fulminating, leads the procession away into the Channel Tunnel

As the ranting voice became a scream
I knew I was reaching the end of the dream,

And the whole gang would vanish utterly
Into one giant under-sea
Collecting-bin known as *History*.

Film Noir

They came from different directions, the man and the mist,
Towards the house. She dragged the window shut
As the mist prowled down from one end of the block
And the man from the other; against whom she ran
To fix the chain on the door. But the mist was in
Before the window closed, and the man was in
Before the chain had slid along the groove.

He set his hat on a table, the mist
Came with it, his gloves went palm-on-palm
On the arm of a chair, his two hands proffered
Their fingers to the mist to be introduced;
And neither he nor she could dare to speak.
She waited as if for her two visitants
To be acquainted first. There was a fourth,

38

There was a fourth, which could neither speak nor move
By definition, the fourth was silence,
The last and deepest reunion for them all.
The silence waited too. The mist sank down
And crept into far corners, knowing this brought
Their faces into focus as they stood.
And neither of them feared enough to scream.

War-thoughts

now that I have returned and that war-thoughts
Have left their places vacant, in their rooms
Come thronging soft and delicate desires . . .

Much Ado About Nothing

This is the day when our brave boys are safely returning.
The flowers and the bunting, which drapes every street, have
been sponsored by Chambers of Commerce to fête their home-
coming, whose victory has rendered our pride and rejoicing
complete. Our boys, too, feel proud – of the courage they
showed for the nation with sheath-knives and missiles.
Their honour will not be put down. Their honour is sacred.
Such honour has been our salvation. The military virtues
are back in town: our boys will have fought with a far
cleaner spirit than others, and not once succumbed to
strange vices in soft, scarlet rooms, in foreign bordellos
frequented unknown to their mothers. Our boys will have
sent them back postcards of classical tombs and Renaissance
chantries.

Their war was our video game. Their privations
were set out in graphics that whirled on the screen, while
mandarins from Defence, with their charts and statistics,
were showing in detail the world that our boys would
have seen. When our boys turn the corner and enter the
square in procession, their feet will stamp once and be
still, the line come to a stop. The scaling of fifes and
bombardment of side-drums will lessen, our hearts miss their
beat as the rifle-butts drop with one crash to the ground.
They will stand up erect (no one falters) while wreaths
of respect are laid over the previous dead; and then
march off again, to break up and disperse to their quarters,
where some of our boys will crawl gratefully off to their
bed.

But others will flourish their swords in
the thirsty environs of bar and casino and dance-hall,
and shout battle-songs; at bus-stops at midnight will
curse – and be cursed by – civilians not proud of our
boys for redressing their wrongs. Their officers, though,
will lie stretched out in exquisite arbours, enhancing
their peace with anthologies of trees; and tonight will
assume elaborate masks for the dancing; and go in for
drawing up battlefield strategies of love; and each delicate
move of love's quarries will show on their sigint com-
puters precisely. Thus, turning up for the Governor's
Reception, one young blood, the bravest, will know
where to find the best beauty and come at the spoils
of his war.

THE AUTOMATIC DAYS

The Days of Hope and Love

Monday morning in the spring, no customers,
And beginning another automatic week,
The Manager, all humorously formal:
'Ladies, I'd like you to meet Beverley!'
– And Beverley shyly walking in and nodding
To Tamsin and Mrs Gurnard, who have worked here
Six months and seven years respectively;
Beverley having been trained upstairs for her role,
Its courtesy and vigilance, told what
To wear and how to wear it, told to look neat
And above all to always smile. And all those things
She learned at school she might as well forget.

In the middle of this floor, most of the day,
Mrs Gurnard sits in a nine-inch-higher-up
Enclosure with her cash desk and credit slips,
From this panoptical vantage being able
To see down lines of dresses in all directions,
And watch the furrowed looks of customers
Holding the garments up against themselves
To wonder how they might look in daylight,
And scanning the length of their bodies to the floor,
And looking in vain for mirrors to flatter them.
She has to keep an eye on everything.
To Beverley Tamsin says, 'Mrs G.'s all right.'

But on Beverley's second day, Tamsin says,
'You think you can laugh and joke with her, and then
She goes all prim and chilly; serious.
Like, she was telling me the Manager
Has this funny way of pronouncing "suppliers",
He says it "supplars". And I laughed and that,
And went on sorting this pile of dresses, when
She turns and says, "You're not at a jumble sale,"
– All sudden and sharp, with a funny look – "You're *not*
At a *jumble* sale." But mostly she's all right.'
They both look covertly at Mrs Gurnard
Where she smiles and hands back someone's credit card.

And what should portend love and hope, the spring,
Does indeed bring the Financial New Year,
And the stocktaking for everyone, closing earlier
The first three afternoons of the previous week;
Which Tamsin finds a bother. Tamsin thinks,
'When it's sold you know it's gone, so why trouble
To count it before you sell it? Tomorrow,
You sell some more, the number's different.
Next week they buy in new stuff for the Sale . . .
I don't like the Manager's jokes, his great long lists
On clipboards, Mrs Gurnard going spare.'
You have to give them time to understand.

The Day of the Asterisk

The music stops in mid-bar on the PA,
So all the customers realise there was music
And wonder what comes now. 'Will Mrs Gurnard
Come to the Manager's office, will Mrs Gurnard
Come to the Manager's office. Thank you.' Click,
And the music starts again. Therefore she swivels
Round to tell Tamsin to stay with the cash desk,
And strides off smiling* down a glade of coats
To do the thing for which she has been thanked.
The customers themselves feel thanked for suffering
A remission of the music which they hardly
Knew they were hearing. Tomorrow is the Sale.

*She smiles at the girl on the cosmetics,
Penned in among the scents and paints and creams,
Who returns her a tanned and haggard look
Expensively reproaching anyone
Who passes, and will not be beautiful.
She smiles through the caféteria swing doors,
And she smiles at Trevor with his agreements,
Imprisoned by some thirty capering screens.
At any second, somewhere in the world,
You can push a flat square button and get the sound
Of an audience screaming with happiness.
She pushes the bell for the Manager's happy smile.

Identity

Next day she wears a square blue disc which says:
                MARY GURNARD
                ASSISTANT MANAGERESS
A few inquisitive customers contrive
To read it, then look up and fit the name
To the face, or *vice versa*. More customers
Interrupt what she's doing with enquiries;
It must be the disc, or something in the way
She stands, or gives instructions to younger people,
Or just seems older . . . Beverley's little disc
Says only BEVERLEY, Tamsin's TAMSIN.
Mrs Gurnard now walks faster everywhere,
Effect of being promoted to be old.

From now on she is one of eleven 'A.M.s',
Men and women; and nearly all the time
The shop is in focus for her. But customers
Are a *problem*, or watching them is; one of
Her big responsibilities the moment
She enters. Being a customer herself
Does not feel natural any more, you go
To other shops, and watch; or wonder who
Is customer and who Security.
Some of the staff are Security as well.
Beverley has a dream that, except for her,
All customers and staff are Security.

Forms of Summer

The eyes of the naked dummy, just shiny-smooth
Head and trunk and legs, no arms as yet,
Which stare over Trevor's shoulder as he humps it
Past other dismembered, hollow legs at
The hosiery counter, posing on small
Balletic, stuck-down toes, are eyes which frown
Reproaching everyone, any way they look.
In their store-room, all the dummies stare like that,
A gallery of smoothness and reproach.
As it passes her, it reproaches Beverley.
It catches her eye and she doesn't like it.
She likes it better when they give it arms.

He is taking it down to the Summer Window.
It will sit there, legs apart, with a traumatised gaze
Through the glass at shoppers passing in the Precinct.
It will be dressed for Summer, and for Sports.
As he turns a corner, almost bumping in-
to Tamsin flinching back against a wall,
He calls out, 'Be like that!' quick, as, a, flash . . .
Someone else carries down arms, and clothes,
To make a woman of it. The sun shines in
On the soft pavane of dust through the display
Of badminton equipment, where she remains
Looking healthy and distraught for seven weeks.

Behaviour of Lifts

The lift-door opens. Trevor, with a trolley,
Grins as he shifts it to let Tamsin in.
She crams between the trolley and the closing
Doors, which have tried to trap her, but draw back
With mechanical respect. At last she is inside,
And down it goes, slowly, the two of them hearing
The music, watching one number go out
And another shine, as they pass groups of faces
On floors where it does not stop. In their silence,
Trevor sees the silver crucifix which lies
On the broad plain of skin above, between, her breasts.
The Ground Floor arrives . . . 'Can you press the Open
                                                                    Doors?'

Going up again it misses a floor and opens
Where nobody is needing to get out;
So there are smiles. Or opens two floors higher,
And is empty to a deputation waiting
As if to receive a visitor, people who say
They are going Down, not Up. The arrow says Up,
The bell has chimed it open, it will not close
Until someone leaps in, yelping, and stabs a button
And leaps out fast, and it works! But through the glass
They see the serenaded vacancy
Refusing to move, insisting it stays and waits.
Then it opens again, like a future, like a grave.

Oral Contact with a Duck

Rise up a brief metal escalator, see
Mrs Gurnard dash into a cubicle,
And dab some powder on her face, and touch
A spot not there this morning, and snatch her bag,
And lift her coat from an alcove and hurry out
Through the suddenly dropping swathe of heat
At the glass doors opening onto the Precinct,
Where, among the concrete pots of late summer flowers,
Goodbody's have put some lime-green litter-bins:
'A Message from Goodbody's: KEEP OUR PRECINCT TIDY!'
– At entirely their own expense. Mrs Gurnard
Drops into one a wrapper from a mint,

And then she goes on with her sandwiches,
And enters the Park by an almost unknown gate,
A small pedestrian gate too narrow
For cars or even horses, used by few,
Where she does not pause to read, on a notice board,
The Regulations, giving opening times
And things not allowed in the Park: no dropping
Of litter, no giving of political speeches,
No playing of musical instruments, no groups
Of more than six persons to play any game
Except on the authorised pitches. She is alone
On this cloudy lunch hour, free of the Summer Skirts,

And a duck walks up towards her, hopefully,
With the arcane, superior look of a species
Not often spotted in the Park, a fowl
Flown in from somewhere else and followed by
A mate in a plumage not to be described
Without a bird book. She undoes her coat,
And the duck appears to scrutinise the disc
She is wearing under it, with her name and role
Punched out in capitals. She calls, and stretches,
And holds out a piece of torn-off buttered crust
To the duck, which stands and . . . stands and . . . Mrs
                                                  Gurnard
Speculates, 'Can you sniff if you have a beak?'

As the duck stands pondering, and Mrs Gurnard
Speaks to it quietly, trying it with the bread,
She seems to sense a moment of inanition,
A second of being mesmerised to nothing . . .
Her stare, as she stares, middle-aged, at the bird
Is like the preoccupation of a child,
Or the acquiescence of senility
In things coming harmlessly close to hand:
A somewhat low point of human consciousness,
A chilly moment when being alive (for her)
Is only being alive to focus clearly
The sniffing beak, and eye, of a strange duck.

The Clearances

The Early Autumn Clearance begins next week,
And no one feels ready for it. 'Back to
School!' still challenges in the window. Tamsin yawns,
While all day long the artificial flowers,
In their most perfectly arranged cascades,
Are spilling out from baskets on golden strings;
Or bogus foliage, standing in wooden troughs
Of artificial soil (each swathe and frond
Of bracken, every stalk and tendril, false),
Is wavering slightly, as the counter fans
Bend slow and cagey faces sightlessly
From side to side, droning all afternoon.

And what floods in when the Clearance opens
Are impotent- and violent-looking people
In anoraks, men and women, with plastic bags,
Who saunter through the glades of Goodbody's
Automatically. Here they are, pressing at
Pink mattresses with the spread-out fingers of
One loose hand; and there they go, turning up
Price labels on bath towels and dropping them,
The newness of everything turns them shabby,
Imperfect persons puzzled by perfect things.
They cannot live up to what they see, and if
They bought it, it would start to live down to them.

Beverley

Beverley has for a moment the madness
Of seeing every happening as unique:
A shot of Tamsin rearranging skirts
With a squeal of hangers, or a nun lifting
A frying pan slowly in the Kitchen Ware
And turning it over, scanning her blurred face
In the shiny base of it. Beverley looks away,
But wants to faint as she sees Mrs Gurnard
Stroll past the TV screens all smiles at Trevor,
And each screen flooding with a farewell crimson
As a jocular cartoon worm wriggles off
Into the sunset, doffing his hat: THE END.

Some of the thoughts that come can be so awful,
She has to go through the China, and past
The Furniture into the Garden Goods, and down
To an extreme hushed corner where older
Assistants render slow help with Sewing Aids,
And out through a green and white Exit. In the Precinct,
She could be any other assistant escaped
For lunch; except it's twenty-five past three . . .
Will she walk up and down to breathe, or just
Walk on not knowing where she might end, until
She looks all wrong down at the bus station
In her working skirt, among shoppers with plastic bags?

Somewhere Else

One Sunday Trevor has asked Tamsin out
For a drive, in the wet, down waterlogged lanes
And narrow open roads over prairie fields
Of sugar beet; and they are lost, with the dusk
Coming on. At a lonely intersection,
Near to a wooden sign they cannot read,
He stops without warning, and an unseen car
Is blaring at them, a front-seat passenger
Is turning to snarl. NO THROUGH ROAD TO THE BASE
Is what the sign says: lights in Amusement Rooms
Shine distantly over chained swings. The heating cools
Too quickly, their windows fog, they can't see out.

Whatever Trevor wanted to make of it,
Whatever Tamsin wondered about, or feared
(What *had* she agreed by coming out at all?)
The day makes the decisions. Water-drops
Run very fast, opaquely, down the windscreen;
And somehow he cannot move his left hand farther
Across than the gear-stick, which, in the deepest thought,
He joggles to and fro. As the land withdraws,
He draws, in the steam on the glass, a nose and eyes
With his forefinger; and one eye runs a tear.
They look out through the face at the looming dark,
And talk about Work between the silences.

The Last of Autumn

On a slack Monday morning (in her dream)
Mrs Gurnard comes in and sees a customer
Paying coins into Tamsin's outstretched fingers.
Tamsin's fingers turn them over onto her palm,
And they transform into toads. Not only that,
But the customer is wearing the Manager's hat
With a square blue disc on it: BEAT THE XMAS RUSH,
And is some peculiar kind of reptile.
Tamsin is also stroking him, or it.
'You are not supposed to stroke a customer,'
She tells Tamsin. Tamsin makes a sign.
Trevor and Beverley only stand and laugh.

On a slack Monday morning, Mrs Gurnard,
Having had a 'frightful night', comes in and sees,
And focuses, only the rain dribbling down
On the windows; she thinks every droplet carries,
Like a shell on its downward racing back,
A small aborted Precinct. And all around,
Xmas is starting up: this year's diaries
(Cheaper since March, and August) all replaced
By next year's; near the typewriters, new shelves
Of gift-packed stationery in pastel boxes;
Mistletoe wrappers round adhesive tape;
Small snowman price tags added to Artist's Pads.

The Sunshine Coffee Lounge

The caféteria has doors made to swing,
Like the doors of a Wild West saloon in a film,
Spectacular to burst through and bellow while
The camera has them swinging shut behind.
A trickle of Xmas customers comes in:
Two women with each other, a short woman
Leading a child not wishing to be led,
A red-bearded man, two Security
With shoulder flashes, and three sixth-form boys.
The cashier slides onto her plastic seat,
The kitchen echoes to a sudden shriek
Of badinage, and the filtered coffee drips.

And the customer with the red beard goes along
The row of pastries, shut into compartments
Which you open by lifting vertical perspex lids.
An eerie glow of striplight is enough
To give his eyes a leer, a ghastly look
As he gazes in, very slow and indecisive,
-to the recesses of a range of trays,
As if there were nothing more melancholic
Than these flat plains of pure confectionery,
And nothing worse than to place some on a plate
With a pair of aluminium tongs, and get
It rung up by a silent, sad cashier.

In the Snow

November: Tamsin, helping to window-dress,
Lifts a large cardboard Santa Claus into a window,
A two-dimensional figure of a bare-
legged blonde in Santa's red hood and gown,
The traditional elderly bringer of gifts
Updated to please an age not given
To reverence for age, but certain to esteem
The gift of sex. She rides a little sleigh,
And she'll be down your flue in a week or two.
Anyone passing might be forgiven
For doing a double-take thinking she was real.
'Her legs must get cold, in the snow like that!'

The reindeer pulling her could not be real,
But the plainclothes Security at Xmas are.
'You need them then more than any other time,'
Says Mrs Gurnard, quoting the Manager.
They go round in the guise of men-in-the-street,
In fur-collared coats, or jeans and anoraks,
Choosing their gifts with young Security wives.
They examine three-piece suites, watch demonstrations,
And ask about the price of foreign soaps
On the cosmetics. They watch the assistants
Most carefully when they go home at Xmas,
Hands deep in pockets clutching children's shoes.

In the Tinsel

Now it's the time for carols, carols, carols,
Incessantly resounding on the PA,
Only pausing to notify lost children
Taken howling to the playroom and left to swim
In seas of coloured balls. Half of the screens
Show Xmas videos of Seasonal Offers;
Snow is falling in them. A tiger walks
To and fro on his hindlegs the length of the Ground Floor,
And draws attention to the Toys Department
With a sandwich board concealing his lack
Of credible features. Mrs Gurnard turns
A young tramp, sleeping, out of the photo booth,

And Tamsin is in the tinsel. In her dream,
She has stolen it from the Interest Rates display
In the Building Society Xmas window,
And draped it round and round her as she walks
Glittering, as she glides, up the Precinct
Like a distraught one of the recent dead
Who make their way half-dazed through the studio
Mists of the hereafter in a film about
People from a wrecked airship touching down
(So they come to learn) in heaven. And Tamsin is
The youngest one, who never should have died.
It's right her boyfriend joins her at the end.

The Automatic Days

And they finally arrived at the grey pit
Between the Xmas rush and the New Year Sales;
Which you could fall into and not be thought of,
And lie there gazing up at a paper bell
Tangled round with bows of artificial silk,
Looking frayed and stained in the draught from the swing doors,
While the days did not draw in and would not draw out,
And the sunsets came cold and frail. Going through
PINE MIRRORS: HUGE REDUCTIONS, Beverley's face
Is reduced to a summary of the months
Since spring; she shakes her hair across its learnt
Grimaces, will she stop for the New Year?

Next day she stops at a particular
Pine Mirror, a line rather hard to sell,
And fixes in it a special rigid stare.
Far away behind her in slow miniature,
She sees Mrs Gurnard and Tamsin listening
While Trevor tells a joke, automatic days
Are passing while she stands there. Everyone
Knows of the moment when you choose between
Yourself and the mirror they give you. Beverley,
Seeing all of Goodbody's waiting for her to move,
Pushes her hair back and controls her lips;
Braces her spirit and walks right on through.